THEN & NOW®

CHARLESTON

Opposite: Kanawha Valley Traction Company employees pose for a photograph in front of the Virginia Street carbarn in 1906. Limited streetcar service began in Charleston in 1888 and expanded throughout the Kanawha Valley by World War I. Bus service replaced the streetcars in 1939. A portion of the carbarn, built in 1903, still stands as part of Goodwill Industries. (Courtesy of Kanawha Valley Regional Transportation Authority.)

CHARLESTON

Billy Joe Peyton

For the beautiful, charming, and talented CJ, who inspires me to be a better person every single day. Thank you for putting up with me—I love you very much.

Copyright © 2010 by Billy Joe Peyton
ISBN 978-0-7385-6674-0

Library of Congress Control Number: 2009933395

Published by Arcadia Publishing
Charleston, South Carolina

Printed in the United States of America

Then and Now is a registered trademark and is used under license from Salamander Books Limited

For all general information contact Arcadia Publishing at:
Telephone 843-853-2070
Fax 843-853-0044
E-mail sales@arcadiapublishing.com
For customer service and orders:
Toll-Free 1-888-313-2665

Visit us on the Internet at www.arcadiapublishing.com

ON THE FRONT COVER: Pictured here are two images of a familiar city landmark and gathering spot. Area residents know it as the Kanawha County Public Library, which has occupied the location at Capitol and Quarrier Streets since 1967. But it was originally erected by the federal government in 1911 as a post office and federal building. (Then image courtesy of Kanawha Valley Regional Transportation Authority; now image courtesy of the author.)

ON THE BACK COVER: Capitol Street was Charleston's main street for most of the 20th century. This is a typical scene when downtown streets bustled with activity. A crowd is gathered on the library plaza in this late-1960s view, while pedestrians in the background shop at familiar local businesses like Cohen Drug and the Peanut Shoppe, which has been selling its goodies from the same location since 1950. (Courtesy of Jerry Waters.)

Contents

Acknowledgments

Many important people contributed to the success of this work. First, I wish to thank family and friends who offered words of encouragement and guidance along the way and cheerfully granted my wishes for solitude as deadlines loomed and my patience waned.

A heartfelt thank-you goes to Stan Cohen, Stan Bumgardner, Richard Andre, Henry Battle, Harriet Hoy, Alice Khoury, Dennis Strawn, and Charles Halstead, who provided material for this work. Other invaluable assistance came from Charleston Newspapers, Kanawha County Public Library, Kanawha Valley Historical and Preservation Society, Kanawha Valley Regional Transportation Authority, West Virginia Department of Transportation, West Virginia State Archives, West Virginia State Historic Preservation Office, and West Virginia University Libraries.

I am deeply grateful to Jerry Waters for kindly allowing me to use his extensive collection of rare and unusual images. He has chronicled Charleston's 20th-century development through photographs that may be viewed at www.mywvhome.com. Unless otherwise noted, all photographs are courtesy of the author. Also, my editor, Amy Perryman, deserves much of the credit for making this a reality. She has been a joy to work with, especially as I stumbled through the steps of preparing electronic images.

As always, my principal supporter and inspiration has been my wife, Christine. I now have time to bake some bread, CJ!

INTRODUCTION

Charleston's history begins with Native Americans, who lived here for thousands of years before Europeans arrived. Nearby salt springs attracted animals, which congregated to take in the precious mineral. Native peoples came to hunt the game and boil the brine to make salt for seasoning and preserving their food. Despite these advantages, few Native Americans lived here when the first Europeans arrived. Charleston's early settlement is rooted in the struggle for control, first between Britain and France and then by colonists who bristled under the crown's oppressive tax policies after the French and Indian War. It was during this growing strife that the first settlers arrived in the Kanawha Valley in 1773. Repeated Shawnee attacks, followed by a British and Native American alliance during the Revolutionary War, drove most early residents back across the mountains.

Displaced citizens appealed to the Virginia government for a military post at the mouth of Elk River, and in 1788, George Clendenin led a group of intrepid settlers to land he owned there. The governor directed him to organize a company of rangers and erect a fort for the frontier defense. Informally called Clendenin's Station, it stood on a high bank near the intersection of present Brooks Street and Kanawha Boulevard. Clendenin's family lived inside the fort, officially designated as Fort Lee for Revolutionary War hero and former Virginia governor Richard Henry Lee. Other cabins stood in the nearby hardwood forest.

At Clendenin's urging, the Virginia Legislature created Kanawha County in November 1788. Clendenin became a delegate to the legislature, where he was later joined by Daniel Boone. In 1794, county officials urged the state to establish a town at the mouth of Elk River. Clendenin volunteered a 40-acre tract of land and named the settlement Charlestown (changed to Charleston) in honor of his father, Charles, who died at Fort Lee. The original town boundary extended to present Capitol Street and included Front Street (Kanawha Boulevard) and Back Street (Virginia Street).

Disillusioned over Charleston's slow growth, George Clendenin sold his land and left the area in 1796. The town had only 100 people by 1810, when Kanawha County's population numbered around 3,900 whites and 350 slaves. But area prospects quickly improved as a result of commercial salt production, which began modestly in 1797. Kanawha salt found its market during the War of 1812, when the United States banned British imports. Fifty-two furnaces lined the Kanawha River above Charleston by 1815; in 1846, production yielded 3.2 million bushels, which led the nation. The industry spurred timbering, coal mining, barrel making, and flatboat construction. It also created immense wealth for some people, but prosperity came at a price. Dirt and smoke from the furnaces fouled the air, and salt-making firmly established slavery in Kanawha County.

To escape the environmental degradation and "rough elements" near the furnaces, prominent salt makers moved their families down to Charleston, where they built large and stately homes. "Beautifully situated and finely ornamented with shade trees," as noted in the *Cincinnati Chronicle* in 1831, Charleston society rapidly matured with churches, newspapers, and schools, and by 1840, it was the mini-metropolis of the Kanawha Valley. The attractive little town found itself at the center of early fighting when the Civil War erupted in 1861. Residents struggled with the hardships of war as delegates from Virginia's western counties met in Wheeling to discuss options for remaining loyal to the Union. Their efforts culminated in the founding of West Virginia in 1863, with Wheeling as the capital.

Political winds shifted drastically after the war when ex-Confederates regained the right to vote. In 1870, they helped elect a Democrat-dominated legislature that moved the capital to Charleston, a village of 3,100 people with no railroad and few hotel rooms. But growth came quickly to the new seat of government. In 1871, the town extended its eastern boundary to Bradford Street; the 100-room Hale House opened and the first gas lights came on the next year, followed by completion of the C&O Railroad and a new bridge over Elk River in 1873. Improvements notwithstanding, state lawmakers considered the Kanawha Valley too isolated and provincial, so they returned the capital to Wheeling in 1875. A statewide referendum finally settled the issue by making Charleston the permanent seat of government. When lawmakers returned in 1885, they occupied a new capitol building in the heart of downtown.

The 1880s ushered in a long period of sustained growth for the city, which was benefitting from reliable river and rail service. By 1900, Charleston had evolved into a small but modern city of around 12,000, with two principal residential areas—one situated along the west bank of Elk River and called Elk City and, after incorporation into the city in 1895, the West Side. Railroading and industry prevailed in this area, and the housing stock tended to be modest in design to accommodate working-class families. As the city expanded, so, too, did the need for adequate housing nearer to the downtown business and political district. In the 1880s, another residential area developed in the prime bottomland east of downtown, known as the East End. Many of its inhabitants owned businesses, held executive positions in banks and industry, or worked in state government just a few blocks away. They built large and stylish homes that reflected their social standing and made the East End the most desirable address in the city.

Beginning in the early 1900s, major developments extended the urban landscape. First, Kelly Axe and Tool factory opened in 1905 on the West Side at Patrick Street. At its peak, it employed over 1,000 workers and produced 40,000 finished tools daily. Then, in 1917, the Libbey-Owens sheet glass plant and an adjacent bottling works opened on the upper South Side in Kanawha City. Charleston experienced unprecedented growth as a center of government, banking, and commerce after World War I; the population reached 40,000 by 1920, as high as 67,000 in 1940, and 85,000 in 1960. Coal mining, manufacturing, and chemical production based on salt and abundant natural gas led the industrial expansion. But rapid growth also had its downside. Urban decay had begun, traffic jams clogged streets, and parking shortages plagued downtown.

Optimistic estimates predicted the city would top 100,000 residents—which never happened. In fact, dramatic changes had the opposite effect. In the 1960s and 1970s, Charleston suffered mounting job losses, urban renewal wiped out large portions of the historic downtown, and interstate highway construction eliminated entire neighborhoods. In 1980, the Libbey-Owens-Ford glass plant and True Temper (formerly Kelly Axe) factory closed. The city's population dropped to 64,000 by 1980. In 1983, shoppers abandoned downtown in favor of the newly opened Town Center Mall. Fortunately, forward-thinking planners opted to locate the mall within walking distance of the old central business district. As a result, the downtown has been revitalized as Charleston Village, where traffic jams are a thing of the past and tree-lined streets shade historic buildings containing an eclectic blend of shops, restaurants, and offices. Today Charleston is a moderate-sized capital city of 50,000 people with a small-town ambience. Gone (but certainly not forgotten) are memorable landmarks such as the Capitol Annex, Kearse Theater, and Greyhound bus station. Charlestonians lament these lost treasures but also have reason to celebrate because much of the historic city survives.

In writing this work, the author seeks to go beyond the more familiar views of Charleston by including some new or forgotten aspects of the city's past. It is hoped that readers will enjoy this humble effort to capture glimpses of our shared heritage and that it will be of interest to local history enthusiasts for years to come.

CHAPTER 1

DOWNTOWN

BEAUTIFULLY SITUATED AND FINELY ORNAMENTED

Spectators gather on May 3, 1892, to watch the cornerstone being laid for the Kanawha County Courthouse. The view is to the northwest across Court Street. Beyond the construction site at Virginia and Court Streets is the 1888 jail, which was replaced with a larger facility during a major expansion that tripled the size of the courthouse in 1924. Charleston's population was around 7,500 and growing at the time. (Courtesy of West Virginia University Libraries.)

Charleston has always been a river city, as depicted here. A pair of four-story buildings dominates the 1896 skyline—the 1892 courthouse at left and 1870 Union School at right—while farms dot the hills north of town. Buildings cantilevered over the riverbank are evidence that waterways were commercial arteries, not recreational amenities. In the modern scene, the courthouse is dwarfed against taller buildings. Haddad Riverfront Park is a focal point of downtown, and Charleston now embraces its river heritage. (Then image courtesy of West Virginia University Libraries.)

This view of Charleston's main street is dominated by overhead utility lines that symbolize a modern turn-of-the-20th-century city. Two lads are crossing Kanawha Street toward the 1885 Ruffner Hotel, before removal of its original Victorian facade. The inn was demolished in 1970 for a parking lot. At Capitol and Kanawha Streets is the distinctive turret of the 1854 Kanawha Valley Bank building. Directly across the street stands the May Shoe Company, a site now occupied by the Union Building. (Then image courtesy of West Virginia University Libraries.)

Bass Jewelers, Frankenberger's, Kanawha Valley Bank, and Schwabe-May are among the businesses that began on Kanawha Street before moving elsewhere. All the structures on the north (left) side between Summers and Capitol Streets fell victim to urban renewal in the early 1960s. In 1969, Charleston National Bank (now Chase Bank) erected the 17-story plaza that now occupies the entire block. It illustrates the worst in 1960s urban design, because the complex turns its back on the river and Capitol Street and its landscaped plaza is inaccessible. (Then image courtesy of Stan Cohen.)

Kanawha Hotel was built between Summers and Virginia Streets in 1903 and expanded in 1907. For six decades, it provided excellent accommodations, but changing tastes and chain hotels led to its closing in 1965. It then found new life as the Charleston Job Corps center for over 30 years. When the Job Corps moved to a new facility outside of town, the end had come. Despite efforts to save it, Kanawha Hotel fell to the wrecking ball in 2003. Fifth Third Bank now occupies the site. (Then image courtesy of Stan Cohen.)

A forgotten area of old Charleston bordered the railroad and warehouse district north of downtown. With the exception of Joe Fazio's Spaghetti House, little evidence remains of the people, black and white, who lived and worked on Dryden Street, Welch Street, Young Street, and other nearby streets some might consider "the wrong side of the tracks." Court and Dryden Streets, pictured in the 1950s, is now a railroad underpass that runs by West Virginia–American Water Company, out of view at left. The warehouse in the distant background is vacant today. (Both images courtesy of Jerry Waters.)

When the permanent state capital moved to Charleston in 1885, lawmakers occupied the massive Victorian building shown here. Fire destroyed this landmark in 1921, and the 20-story Kanawha Valley Building was erected on the site in 1929. Prior to construction of Laidley Tower in the 1980s, it was the tallest office structure in West Virginia. Kanawha Valley Bank moved to One Valley Square (now BB&T Square) in 1976, and SunTrust Bank now owns the Kanawha Valley Building. The southwest corner of the old capitol lawn is preserved as the Lee Street Triangle. (Then image courtesy of West Virginia University Libraries.)

The old Baptist Temple was built at the northeast corner of Washington and Capitol Streets in 1904. Constructed of distinctive red sandstone, the structure was demolished when the church moved to its present location at Morris and Quarrier Streets in 1925. The cornerstone from the 1904 church is in front of the newer Baptist Temple. A filling station occupied the site for many years before the current building was constructed as a bar and restaurant in the 1970s. It now contains FedEx Kinko's and the offices of WQCW-TV. (Then image courtesy of Stan Cohen.)

This view of a 1979 Sternwheel Regatta parade features the popular Beni Kedem Motor Corps on their vintage Cushman scooters. The J. C. Penney and Montgomery Ward department stores date from the 1950s. Both relocated to Town Center Mall in 1983, while the Diamond department store in the background operated from 1927 until 1983. The Penney building has been rehabilitated as Davis Square for state offices, the West Virginia Department of Health and Human Resources occupies the Diamond building, and the Ward's store is an office complex called Geary Plaza. (Then image courtesy of Jerry Waters.)

At least eight downtown movie theaters have existed in the past century, and two still operate. One is Park Place Stadium Cinemas, a modern multiplex at 600 Washington Street. The other is Capitol Plaza Theatre, the city's sole surviving vintage movie palace. Originally a vaudeville house that opened as the Plaza Theatre in 1912, it was redone for films as Capitol Theater in 1921. The Capitol Plaza, which miraculously survived the mass extermination of vintage theaters in the 1980s, has been restored and is now owned by West Virginia State University. (Then image courtesy of Stan Cohen.)

Park Pontiac was a well-known auto dealership that opened in 1941 at 222 Dickinson Street. Company president W. B. Sowers pledged to remain open on a 24-hour basis, seven days a week. With U.S. involvement in World War II looming, it is not known how long he kept his pledge. The large brick building in the background is the old Coyle and Richardson department store. (Then image courtesy of Jerry Waters.)

A Saturday afternoon stroll through the 200 block of Capitol Street in 1960 was a buyer's paradise—four shoe stores, Cox's, Lance's, Kresge's, Woolworth's, Lord's, Embees, McCrory's, and a host of other shopping options. In the early view, Mary Jane Shoes has modernized its storefront with aluminum panels and large stylized lettering in an attempt to emulate the appearance of increasingly popular suburban strip malls. Capitol Street, like main streets nationwide, lost the battle for shoppers by the 1980s. (Then image courtesy of Kanawha County Public Library.)

New Deal efforts to battle the Depression included the Works Progress Administration, which funded public works projects to renew the nation's infrastructure. Charleston residents approved a levy for matching WPA funds to erect a new bridge over Kanawha River. The historic 1937 view shows the South Side Bridge as it nears completion. Changes are apparent in the modern view, including the South Side Expressway. The post and rail fence in the foreground still exists, owing to the durability (and toxicity) of creosoted railroad ties. (Then image courtesy of Kanawha County Public Library.)

In the era before packaged beer and industry domination by national brands, local breweries made and distributed the beverage. Charleston had several breweries between the 1880s and 1917, including the Lion, Slack, DeGruyter, Peyman, and Kanawha Brewing companies. Kanawha Brewing was founded in 1906 at Bullitt Street and Welch Street (now Piedmont Road) with annual production totaling 50,000 barrels. The brewery site is now the BB&T Operations Center. Nothing remains of the brewery building. (Then image courtesy of Paul Marshall.)

The corner of Capitol and Lee Streets has been a busy location since at least 1870. In the 1946 view, the southwest corner of the old capitol lawn has been transformed into the Lee Street Triangle, and the National Bank of Commerce occupies the 1907 Coyle and Richardson Building at the southeast corner of Capitol and Lee Streets. Most recently, it was the location of Charleston Bagel. On the opposite side of the street is the Odd Fellows Building, longtime home of Capital City Commercial College. Delfine's Jewelry currently occupies the first floor. (Then image courtesy of Kanawha County Public Library.)

In the 1930s, the area north of downtown near the railroad was a mixed-use residential and wholesale district. The young girl is standing at Welch Street (now Piedmont Road) and Young Street. Folks like her who lived here struggled constantly with the noise and grime of the steam engines. Today the houses are gone and warehouses have been adapted for other uses. In the foreground is the parking lot of Habitat for Humanity's ReStore; behind it at right stands the Diamond Ice and Coal Company. (Both images courtesy of Jerry Waters.)

Politics always takes center stage in Charleston, especially in an election year. In 1920, the Republican headquarters was conveniently located on State Street (now Lee Street), just west of the state capitol. A few months after this image was made, the capitol, visible in the background, burned. Wilson's Café and Aunt B's Bakery currently occupy the old Piggly Wiggly grocery store. State voters did indeed support the Republican ticket in the 1920 election, the first one in which women could vote. (Then image courtesy of West Virginia State Archives.)

Long considered the naughty sibling to family-friendly Capitol Street, Summers Street once featured a healthy blend of adult-oriented entertainment and wholesome fare. This 1939 view includes the Greyhound bus terminal, designed by Charleston resident and Atlantic Greyhound architect George D. Brown in 1936. Brown conceptualized the streamline look for about 50 terminals throughout the Southeast. Two doors down is Kearse Theater, which is showing *Wife, Husband and Friend*, starring Loretta Young. Every building visible to Quarrier Street was demolished in the 1980s. (Then image courtesy of Jerry Waters.)

A thriving African American residential and commercial district existed north of Washington Street during the Jim Crow era. The 1940 image features the 1907 Knights of Pythias Building at Washington and Dickinson Streets. It included a lodge hall, Gem Pharmacy, Mutual Savings and Loan, East Side Lunch, a YMCA for blacks, and the office of John C. Norman, a prominent African American architect. To the east stood The Block and Hotel Ferguson. The Knights of Pythias Building was demolished in the late 1950s; the site is now a parking lot and drive-in bank. (Then image courtesy of West Virginia State Archives.)

The 1903 Beaux Arts–style Capitol Annex was built at Hale and State (Lee) Streets in 1903 to provide additional space for expanding state government. After the capitol moved to the East End in 1932, all state offices moved out, and the annex housed Morris Harvey College until 1947 and the Kanawha County Public Library until 1966. It was razed in 1967 to make room for Commerce Square (now Huntington Square), a 17-story building constructed by the National Bank of Commerce in the international style. Its granite exterior is adorned with a bronze sculpture by Milton Horn. (Then image courtesy of Stan Cohen.)

Charleston National Bank constructed this seven-story building in 1906 at the northwest corner of Capitol and Quarrier Streets, which did not extend west to Summers Street until 1958. When the bank moved to Charleston National Plaza (now Chase Bank) in 1969, the old building was demolished and Quarrier Street was widened to its current configuration. The city's first McDonald's opened here in 1974 and closed in the 1990s. Two other restaurants have operated on this corner since then. (Then image courtesy of Jerry Waters.)

In the 1930s, the Cox-Morton Company sold DeSoto and Plymouth vehicles from this location at the northwest corner of Goshorn and Virginia Streets, a block that it shared with the courthouse. The dealership moved north across Virginia Street in 1937 to a new and larger facility, where it sold petroleum products from Elk Refinery along with tires, car radios, bicycles, and automobiles. Today the site includes a small green space and parking for the courthouse. (Then image courtesy of Jerry Waters.)

HOTEL FLEETWOOD, CHARLESTON, W. VA.

Charleston has had a number of popular and stylish downtown hotels. One of the earliest was Hotel Fleetwood, established in 1909 by Charleston dentist Dr. Fleetwood Butts. It hosted prominent guests in its prime but suffered an inglorious end as a low-rent dive. The hotel closed in 1955, but the building survived into the 1990s. Its demolition created an undesirable void in the middle of revitalized Capitol Street, prompting city officials to design and erect an attractive fence and landscaping to mask the parking lot behind.

In this 1950s view, all of the original late-1800s buildings still stand on the north side of Kanawha Boulevard; however, within a decade, urban renewal had taken everything west of Capitol Street. WKNA radio station (950 AM) went on the air in 1947 and became WKAZ in 1957. It played a Top 40 format in the 1960s, then became WQBE-AM-FM and adopted a country western format in 1984. The old Franklin Café has been a series of bars, from the Charleston Athletic Club to the Sound Factory. (Then image courtesy of West Virginia University Libraries.)

Otmer, Roma, and Walter Young opened this diner, with ladies invited, in 1932 at 1022 Quarrier Street. They later added a second dining car, and it became Twin Diners restaurant. In 1947, the Youngs built Quarrier Diner, a classic of art deco design with structural glass facade. They also built the Ott Building on Dunbar Street, named for Otmer (Ott) Young. It housed the Hotel Ulysses, as indicated by the faint sign visible in the *c.* 1935 view. Both the Quarrier Diner (later Young's Food House) and the Ott Building still stand, but both are vacant. (Then image courtesy of Harriet Hoy.)

This 1891 photograph is an early view of the northeast intersection of Capitol and Quarrier Streets. The pictured building, the first modern one on the block, was constructed by Coyle and Richardson as a dry goods store about 1890 and later became the second home of Kanawha Banking and Trust. The historic view reveals much about Charleston at the time—Capitol Street is still a rural lane and not yet a bustling commercial center. In the modern view, the building has doubled in size. It serves as offices now. (Then image courtesy of Kanawha County Public Library.)

For seven decades, the Charleston YMCA served the community with a variety of health, fitness, and recreational programs. Built in the Italian Renaissance style, it stood on a lot donated by industrialist Henry Gassaway Davis in 1907. A new and modern YMCA opened on the hills north of town in 1981, and the old Y was subsequently demolished. The only clue to the site's past is the statue of Henry Gassaway Davis that formerly graced the building's entrance. Surrounding the statue is a public green space called Davis Park in his honor. (Then image courtesy of Stan Cohen.)

One of Charleston's enduring landmarks is the 1911 Alderson-Stephenson Building, the tallest office building in West Virginia when built. The structure is commonly called the Union Building because it originally housed the Union Trust Company. What makes it truly unique is its location on the river side of Kanawha Boulevard. Several blocks of buildings had stood alongside it prior to 1938, but boulevard construction eliminated all others. Apparently, only the high cost of its demolition spared the Union Building. It is difficult to imagine the Charleston skyline without it today. (Then image courtesy of West Virginia University Libraries.)

This *c.* 1978 photograph captures the last of the notorious beer joints in the 200 block of Summers Street—a section where the smell of stale beer and cigarette smoke permeated the air. Summers Street could not totally shake its reputation as a seedy strip until all the old haunts met the wrecking ball, which occurred in the 1980s. Slack Plaza, ground-level parking, and office buildings now cover the site. (Then image courtesy of Jerry Waters.)

In 1958, the Charleston Civic Center opened as the state's largest sports arena. Built on a garbage dump near Elk River, it officially held 7,000 people—but rock concerts brought in far more through "festival seating." It hosted the likes of Elvis Presley, Jimi Hendrix, the NBA, college and high school basketball contests, and more. In 1980, the city upgraded the facility with a new coliseum and convention hall. The modern photograph shows the original facade and roof peak protruding above the addition.

The 100 block of Capitol Street is Charleston's oldest, with many buildings dating to the 1880s. Silver Brand Clothes operated in the *c.* 1880 Gates Building (108–110 Capitol Street) in the 1970s. Constructed by Charles Gates for his grocery business, it is a fine example of a late-19th-century eclectic commercial property. After the mall opened in the 1980s, owners restored the building's facade to its simple elegance. The Gates Building is listed on the National Register of Historic Places as part of the Downtown Historic District. (Then image courtesy of National Park Service.)

Although it only existed for about 25 years, the 1967 West Virginia Building and Loan Association headquarters was noteworthy for its unusual contemporary open-face design that featured a surrounding portico of concrete pedestals. Charleston architect Henry Elden designed the building at the northwest corner of Quarrier and Court Streets, and H. B. Agsten was the contractor. The building's short life ended at the hands of a Bob Evans restaurant, which itself succumbed to the recent redevelopment of the parcel as headquarters for Brickstreet Insurance.

Traffic is creeping eastward along U.S. 21 and 60 in this *c.* 1950 rainy-day view of the 700 block of Lee Street between Broad Street (Leon Sullivan Way) and Brooks Street. Homes that existed in the neighborhood at the time would appear to be gone now, but many survive behind their modern commercial facades. The background in the early view is dominated by the Capitol Annex and in the modern view by its replacement, Commerce Square (now Huntington Square). (Then image courtesy of West Virginia University Libraries.)

Taylor Books, an independent bookstore, café, art gallery, and boutique, opened in 1995 at 226 Capitol Street. Resisting the trend of vanishing independent booksellers, Taylor Books is a cornerstone for downtown revitalization and a favorite hangout for area residents. By contrast, the 1970s image depicts the same locale in its last days as a retail destination, when historic buildings had been modernized with false fronts to mimic a suburban strip mall. (Then image courtesy of Jerry Waters.)

Fife Street, really an alley, is named for 19th-century landowner Julia Fife. It is the biggest little street in Charleston, a popular mid-block thoroughfare between Capitol and Summers Streets. Fife Street Shoe Shop and Kanawha Coin Shop were two prevalent businesses in the 1970s view, and they remain so today. Fife Street received a significant makeover in the 1980s with vintage streetlights and brick paving, as it became a critical connector between the mall and downtown. It was also rechristened as Brawley Walkway in honor of longtime educator Harry Brawley. (Then image courtesy of Jerry Waters.)

The *c.* 1910 view depicts a bustling 200 block of Capitol Street. Coyle and Richardson began in 1890 in the corner building, the first in the block to be built. Schwabe and May operated in this block for four decades before moving elsewhere. The longtime clothing retailer opened on Kanawha Street in 1880 and closed for good on Capitol Street in 2008. Other notable retailers in this block included Charleston Hardware, O. J. Morrison's, and McCrory's. Nearly all of the buildings in the early view still exist, many converted to offices. (Then image courtesy of Stan Cohen.)

2

EAST END

CHOICE RESIDENTIAL LOTS
ON GRAND CITY STREETS

Conveniently located on the streetcar line less than a mile east of downtown, the East End developed into a densely populated residential neighborhood by 1910. A tour of the area today includes examples of every major American residential building type that emerged between 1880 and 1940. (Courtesy of Stan Cohen.)

Kanawha Street has been the main east-west route through Charleston since the earliest days. Prominent salt makers began building their estates along the river in the 1820s, and eventually over two dozen grand homes bordered the tree-lined route into town. Over time, many of the stately residences were lost to new development, and they continue to be under siege. The three homes in the *c.* 1905 view still stand, but modern development is encroaching on the scene. (Then image courtesy of Stan Cohen.)

Beginning in the 1880s, the East End became the preferred address for affluent Charlestonians. This view of the 1100 block of Virginia Street features the corner residence of oil operator and newspaperman Moses Donnally. Near the middle of the block are the Virginia Street Temple and Philip Frankenberger residence next door. When the Jewish congregation built a new temple on Kanawha Boulevard in 1960, WCHS-TV/Radio bought and razed the temple. The station then moved into the Frankenberger home, which still exists beneath a modern addition. (Then image courtesy of Stan Cohen.)

Fr. Joseph Stenger organized Charleston's first Catholic church in an old home in 1866. In 1897, he dedicated the current building as Church of the Sacred Heart, now known as the Sacred Heart Co-Cathedral. A recent addition has included an enlarged vestry and gathering space with new landscaped courtyard that nicely complements the cathedral's Romanesque architecture. Later development affiliated with the church includes Charleston Catholic High School and Sacred Heart Grade School. (Then image courtesy of Stan Cohen.)

About 100 years separate these images of homes in the East End Historic District, established in 1988. The historic district includes a wide variety of American architectural styles. From left to right are the c. 1910 American Four Square residence of Frankenberger's vice president, Henry Kleeman; the 1906 Spanish Revival home of Addison Scott, a civil engineer who supervised construction of the first locks and dams on Kanawha River; and the 1907 neoclassical revival dwelling of plumbing merchant Solomon Myers. (Then image courtesy of Stan Cohen.)

Folks are participating in the 1933 Elks Convention along Shrewsbury Street in this view. All-black Garnet High School, which operated from 1928 to 1956, stands in the background. To the south was The Block and Hotel Ferguson, centers of black social life. This vibrant African American neighborhood vanished because of outside influences; its demise began with elimination of black-owned businesses following desegregation, then urban renewal and interstate highway construction finished it off. The neighborhood is all but gone in the modern view, except for one home and Garnet Career Center. (Then image courtesy of West Virginia State Archives.)

Area residents know Laidley Field but not necessarily the original 1915 facility, with wooden bleachers, grass field, and brick wall, that stood until 1978. In the image above, the scoreboard announces the Charleston Rockets' 24-7 victory over the Toronto Rifles in the 1965 Continental Football League Championship. In the background are Piedmont Road and hillside homes demolished to build the interstate highway. The current University of Charleston Stadium at Laidley Field is a modern facility; a portion of the old wall is all that survives after a 1978 reconstruction.

Houses of worship are important cultural components of any neighborhood. East End churches all have interesting histories, but only one has literally risen from the ashes. In 1969, a disastrous fire destroyed the beautiful 1911 Christ Church United Methodist at Quarrier and Morris Streets shown in the 1950s view. The congregation rebuilt in the Brutalist style that gracefully incorporates traditional cut-stone elements and modern roughcast concrete. (Then image courtesy of Stan Cohen.)

Designed and built by the Davidson Brothers of Charleston in 1908, this lovely residence at 1509 Quarrier Street is a vernacular interpretation of a Swiss chalet. It was constructed for Judge Ira Robinson, who served in the West Virginia Senate and was chief justice of the state supreme court. Homes during this period were built to last, often with tile roofs, hardwood trim, and stained-glass windows. Even front doors exhibit master craftsmanship. One hundred years old, this home remains as solid as the day it was built. (Then image courtesy of West Virginia University Libraries.)

The 1962 photograph of Laidley Street was made prior to the demolition of the entire block to build the Charleston House Holiday Inn. Buckeye Loans occupied the large corner building with the Kanawha Hotel looming behind, while the building at right housed Crowder's Watch Repair and Dan J. Popp Hardware and Leather Goods. Popp, along with his famous horse mannequin named Prince, had just moved to 610 Capitol Street, where Prince stood proudly in the front window for many years. Partially visible at left in both views is Woodrum's Furniture, now Wells Fargo Insurance. (Both images courtesy of Jerry Waters.)

Dr. William A. McMillan opened his first hospital in the city in 1913. He later moved into a building at Morris and Lee Street on the East End. McMillan Hospital started with 46 rooms and was later enlarged to a 110-bed facility with a nursing school. The hospital merged with Charleston General in 1971 and became part of Charleston Area Medical Center (CAMC). Afterward, the building was sold and demolished. Ramsey Eye Care operates an optometry clinic on the site today. (Then image courtesy of Jerry Waters.)

America's love affair with the automobile kicked into high gear after World War II. M. R. Wallace capitalized on that relationship and built the Marvin Midtown Motor Hotel, which opened in 1960 with a single 30-room building. Later additions included a front-facing open glass restaurant and office, ell wing at the back, and swimming pool. The Marvin remained open through the 1980s but lost its guests to chain establishments. It is now owned by Riverview Presbyterian Church.

After the disastrous 1921 fire destroyed the 1885 capitol, lawmakers chose to rebuild on a new site in the upper East End. Twenty years after Cass Gilbert designed the capitol building, his son, Cass Gilbert Jr., was hired to design Building 3, commonly known as the Department of Motor Vehicles building. Completed in 1952, it complements the capitol and does not detract at all from its grandeur. Young trees that surrounded the fountain circle in the 1950s have grown into majestic oaks now.

From 1964 to 1968, Laidley Field was home to the Charleston Rockets, who played one year in the United Football League before joining the Continental Football League. Fans may recall this red, white, and blue Air Force rocket parked in the end zone on game days. Houses on Elizabeth Street and Piedmont Road in the 1965 image no longer exist. Residents who lived close to the field could watch games from the comfort of their windows or rooftops.

Charlestonians endured numerous traffic delays during interstate highway construction. When work was complete in 1975, many old and familiar routes had been permanently altered or even obliterated. Access to Piedmont Road, the convenient shortcut between East and West Charleston, had been altered. Some streets no longer extended to it, and the road itself was relocated to accommodate the elevated highway. The 1969 photograph of old Piedmont Road east of Slack Street was made prior to the start of demolition for the highway. (Then image courtesy of Jerry Waters.)

Many of Charleston's old hospitals were small, privately owned affairs. One such facility was Mountain State Hospital, which operated in an elegant home formerly owned by Mayor Grant Hall at 1301 Virginia Street. Mountain State opened in 1921 with 120 beds, two operating rooms, a delivery room, and a nursing school. The hospital merged with Charleston Memorial and then closed in 1971. It then became a nursing home before being bought and razed by the Eye and Ear Clinic in 2005. It is now a parking lot for the clinic.

Old Piedmont Road connected Slack and Greenbrier Streets pre-interstate, and it passed several intersecting roads along the way. The 1969 view is at Stadium Place, named for its location in proximity to Laidley Field. The old north wall around Laidley Field is partially visible on the right in the older photograph. Homes pictured above Piedmont Road are gone in the modern image, and the intersection at Stadium Place has been realigned to make room for the modern elevated highway. (Then image courtesy of Jerry Waters.)

The 1700 block of Washington Street, between Duffy and Greenbrier Streets, contained many small businesses, such as Swan Café, Blue Room Beauty Salon, and Frankel's Drug Store. Pictured in front of Capitol Variety Shop at 1708 Washington Street around 1945 are owners Haseeba and Paul Zakaib (on left) and family members Edward and Freda Baz. Capitol Variety Shop remained open until 1971, when it finally gave way to expansion of the Capitol Complex. Nothing remains of the 1700 block today. (Then image courtesy of Alice Khoury.)

When the governor's mansion was completed in 1925, Duffy Street intersected the boulevard to the east of the mansion. In 1946, the state relocated it farther east to create a larger lawn for the mansion and allow for a private driveway in back. This 1946 photograph featuring unidentified protestors near the old Duffy Street–Kanawha Boulevard intersection reveals some interesting details about old Duffy Street. The old curb cut and corner post are visible, but fill has obliterated the former Duffy Street location, where landscaping is lacking. Duffy Street was later eliminated completely. (Then image courtesy of West Virginia University Libraries.)

Charleston's East End is a diverse neighborhood, and much of the area north of Washington Street developed as an industrial district as a result of the railroad. Interspersed among the warehouses and freight buildings were local hangouts like Bernie's at the north end of Broad Street (now Leon Sullivan Way). In the pre-interstate view, a parade float passes the New York Central and B&O Freight Station. Behind the buildings on the left was the Kanawha and Michigan freight depot, which has been rehabilitated as Capitol Market. (Both images courtesy of Jerry Waters.)

CHAPTER 3

WEST SIDE

PERFECTLY LEVEL AND WELL DRAINED WITH CONVENIENT ACCESS

In 1883, the Ohio Central Railroad built the first rail bridge over Elk River. It eventually proved inadequate to handle larger locomotives, so a more substantial span was constructed adjacent to it in 1906. Laborers are working under the watchful eye of company officials, as onlookers watch from the bridge superstructure and the adjacent span. The century-old structure still carries train traffic, and the 1883 Whipple truss is being considered for a proposed rail-trail. (Courtesy of Charles Halstead and Dennis Strawn.)

"Think global and shop local" is a popular slogan today. Charlestonians have been buying locally grown produce for decades, as this 1950s photograph shows. For several decades, Patrick Street between Seventh Avenue and Washington Street was the Patrick Street Market, the place to get seasonal fresh vegetables, local dairy products, and poultry. Meanwhile, other open-air vendors offered handmade goods that ranged from chairs to pottery. Today shoppers flock to Capitol Market at the north end of Capitol Street for fresh local produce. (Then image courtesy of Jerry Waters.)

Many of the city's old neighborhood schools no longer exist. Among those that have disappeared is Elk Elementary School, which stood at Bigley Avenue and Ash Street. It opened on the present site of the Bigley Avenue Little League field in 1899 and fell victim to interstate construction around 1970. Old-timers will recall that the ball fields used to be in a low flood-prone area near Garrison Avenue and Crescent Road. The present fields are on higher ground.

Charleston got its first streetcar suburb in 1907, when developer Steele Hawkins Sr. started selling lots to folks who wanted an "exclusive country home in a community of handsome residences." He called the development Edgewood, and a streetcar line connected it to downtown. In the *c.* 1910 photograph, the streetcar is passing Edgewood Cave. Motorists traveling up Edgewood Drive can still trace the old trolley right-of-way to the top of the hill. (Then image courtesy of Stan Cohen.)

In this historic 1950s view of the 1500 block of West Washington Street, all the traditional neighborhood businesses are here: the Smokehouse grill, Pile Hardware, Thaxton Drugs, Cunningham Cleaners, Fulknier Hardware, and the West Theater. Most of the buildings in this block still stand, but only two of the businesses survive—the Smokehouse restaurant, which has been at the same location since 1949, and Pile Hardware, now located a block west. (Then image courtesy of West Virginia Department of Transportation.)

The first rail line reached the West Side in 1883. As railroads became more plentiful, West Siders grew accustomed to navigating hazardous railroad crossings and waiting in traffic as trains rumbled past. The late-1940s photograph shows a busy Lee Street crossing near the intersection of Washington Street and Edgewood Drive. Much has changed in the modern view, like the recent addition of a nearby Wendy's and Walgreens, but trains still rumble past the railroad crossing here. (Then image courtesy of West Virginia Department of Transportation.)

In the 1800s, a turnpike crossed Elk River on a suspension bridge and passed through Elk City. At Kanawha Two Mile, pictured here, the Point Pleasant Turnpike went left and Parkersburg Turnpike followed the right fork. In the 1900s, the route became West Washington Street, and motorists still either went left on U.S. 35 or right on U.S. 21 at this intersection. The Pure Oil station shown in the 1947 image is gone, but the site is still a crossroads for local traffic, going to Sissonville on the right or Dunbar on the left. (Then image courtesy of West Virginia Department of Transportation.)

The early photograph depicts rush hour traffic at mid-century. In this case, a steady stream of vehicles is traveling on Patrick Street, perhaps exacerbated by workers leaving the nearby True Temper plant at the base of Patrick Street Bridge. Meanwhile, billboards advertise two familiar West Side businesses—Purity Maid Bakery and Valley Bell Dairy. Purity Maid closed years ago, while Valley Bell remains in business on Lee Street. Traffic has eased considerably in the modern view. (Then image courtesy of West Virginia Department of Transportation.)

The far western end of the West Side, confusingly called North Charleston, is a predominantly working-class neighborhood. Woodward Branch (or Drive) is a residential district of North Charleston and principal feeder route to Washington Street. In 1946, the intersection of old Washington Street and Woodward Drive was a local commercial hub with two service stations, a local grocery, North Charleston Hardware, and Starcher Baptist Church. Existing buildings look much the same now, but their uses have changed. (Then image courtesy of West Virginia Department of Transportation.)

For most of the 20th century, West Siders attended one of two public junior high schools. One was Lincoln Junior High. Lincoln's intense rival was Woodrow Wilson Junior High, which stood on Garvin Avenue. Wilson was built in 1925 in response to a growing population. Both junior highs closed when Capital High School opened in 1989. Lincoln stood until 1990 on Delaware Avenue, where Kroger is now, while Wilson was demolished in the 1990s. Unity Village Apartments occupy the site now. (Then image courtesy of Richard Andre and Stan Cohen.)

The Edgewood streetcar right-of-way ran beside the existing road up Edgewood Drive to its terminus beyond Edgewood County Club. At the end of the line stood Edgewood Park, a popular amusement park that opened in 1907. Park structures were situated just over the hill from the platform, which stood at the point where Edgewood Drive begins its descent to Garrison Avenue. (Then image courtesy of Stan Cohen.)

This 1944 view is looking north at Spring Street just beyond the bridge over Elk River. Wholesaler Hudson Distributing Company moved to this location along the New York Central Railroad tracks in 1941. The partially visible one-story building under construction just beyond the tracks at right is Hissom Tabernacle, a local church founded by Rev. Earl Hissom in 1939. Today Hissom family members remain involved in the ministry, and services are still held in the tabernacle building. (Then image courtesy of West Virginia Department of Transportation.)

Elk Banking Company started business in a dry goods store at Charleston and Virginia Streets (now West Washington Street and Tennessee Avenue, respectively) in 1903. It quickly outgrew the space and in 1905 moved to a new building across the street. In 1923, the bank became Charleston Trust Company, and 10 years later, it went into receivership because of the Depression. The building houses offices on the upper floors and has had a number of retail establishments on the ground floor, including Boll Furniture for many years.

This 1944 photograph may not be immediately recognizable as the railroad crossing at West Washington Street and Maryland Avenue. A Fleet Wing gas station is at left, while Carr Street (now Greendale Drive) joins Washington just beyond the truck parked on right. Along the commercial strip today is Tobacco Express occupying the old Shop-A-Minit, Trax nightclub, and Momma Rosa's Pizzeria, formerly a Hardee's and Burger Chef before that. Abbott Sunoco, at the intersection of Greendale Drive, closed several years ago. (Then image courtesy of West Virginia Department of Transportation.)

In days past, most neighborhoods had a corner grocery store. Parents used to send their children on foot or by bike to buy staples, and cheap candy was always an incentive to go. This 1926 photograph is of Mace Grocery, at Pennsylvania Avenue and Cora Street. Just around the corner, on Bigley Avenue, stood Fitch Drug Store and Harper's Hardware. Neighborhood establishments such as these are scarce today. The building here has been enlarged and altered. (Both images courtesy of Jerry Waters.)

Bigley School was built in 1907 on Bigley Avenue at Glen Street. It served the educational needs of a community that was mostly obliterated by interstate construction, as was the school. Its handsome brick styling was common at the time, and several area schools of the same vintage bore a resemblance to it. Bigley School stood about where the Washington Street exit on I-64 West is today. (Then image courtesy of Stan Cohen.)

SOUTH SIDE

FEW RIVALS AS A GREAT INDUSTRIAL CENTER

The unmistakable smokestacks of the Libbey-Owens-Ford glass plant place this 1960s scene at Fifty-fifth Street and MacCorkle Avenue in Kanawha City. A young entrepreneur serves cold drinks by Gay's Hardware—one of about two dozen neighborhood hardware stores in Charleston at the time. Nearby businesses included a barbershop, Childress Maytag, and CIO Union Hall, which represented glass workers. Closure of the glass plant in 1980 and construction of Kanawha Mall (now Shops at Kanawha) anchored redevelopment of the upper South Side. (Courtesy of Jerry Waters.)

Access to the South Side received a boost when MacCorkle Avenue was widened in the 1930s, making it a magnet for development geared to the emerging car culture. Merchants in the 3900 block of MacCorkle enticed shoppers with parking in front of their stores, and cruising the strip became a popular pastime for area teens. Barely visible in the background of the 1950 view is Kanawha Village Apartments, a privately funded 174-unit complex built in 1939. To provide adequate tenant parking, the owners widened Venable Avenue by 10 feet. (Then image courtesy of West Virginia University Libraries.)

Charlestonians like their baseball, and in 1910, the first professional team debuted in the city. In 1916, Kanawha Park was built at Thirty-fifth Street and MacCorkle Avenue, with Kanawha City Bridge providing easy access from downtown. A new park, named for area baseball promoter Walter ("Watt") Powell, opened on the site in 1948. Watt Powell Park hosted hundreds of sporting events, but it grew obsolete and a new East End park replaced it in 2005. The venerable Watt Powell Park was ultimately demolished, and redevelopment plans are pending. (Then image courtesy of Stan Cohen.)

This unusual postcard view of the Libbey-Owens glass plant dates from around 1920. It includes the landmark smokestacks and water tower, along with a railroad spur line that ran from the plant to the C&O main line. It also features another interesting detail—the brick office in the foreground may well be the only surviving remnant of the old glass plant complex. The old eastern end of the plant now contains a Kroger's, Gabriel Brothers, and the Shops at Kanawha. (Then image courtesy of Stan Cohen.)

Charleston annexed much of the South Side in 1929, and development was in full swing when a photographer shot this view at the corner of Fortieth Street and Staunton Avenue in the late 1930s. Residents of this modern Kanawha City neighborhood would soon enjoy paved streets made possible through an infusion of WPA funds. Seven decades later, landscaping has matured and a house occupies the previously empty lot at the northeast corner of the intersection. (Then image courtesy of West Virginia State Archives.)

Charleston Memorial Hospital, built in 1951 on a former golf course in Kanawha City, was named in honor of West Virginia soldiers who died in World War II. In 1982, it merged with other area hospitals to become Charleston Area Medical Center's Memorial Division. The hospital has expanded since becoming headquarters for the Robert C. Byrd Health Sciences Center at West Virginia University, and it functions as a state-of-the-art facility. A small portion of the original roof and brick exterior wall are visible near the center of the modern photograph.

Charleston Memorial Hospital, Charleston, West Virginia

Building the state capitol complex on the East End necessitated the removal of 65 houses in 1923. Some of the affected properties were demolished, but at least 12 were moved across Kanawha River to Beachview, the development named for a nearby bathing beach. Moving the houses proved a monumental task but one the John Eichleay Jr. Company of Pittsburgh successfully completed. The two images, made about 85 years apart, show the South Ruffner Street landing site for the "mobile" homes. Newer homes dot the riverbank in the modern view. (Then image courtesy of Historic Glenwood Foundation.)

Once the moved houses reached South Ruffner Street, they were lined up for placement on designated lots. The 1923 photograph shows the moved homes following their voyage across the river. Today the sidewalk and remnant of front steps are the last tangible evidence of homes demolished for expanded parking at University of Charleston's Blackwell Field. Several former East End homes exist on an adjacent street. On the hill in the modern picture is Imperial View Apartments. (Then image courtesy of Historic Glenwood Foundation.)

Construction of a bridge across Kanawha River in 1891 connected downtown with the C&O Depot and helped open the sparsely settled South Hills area for growth. It also improved downtown access for the relatively few residents of Fernbank, the neighborhood above the South Side. A dirt trail wound its way up the hill a century ago, while Louden Heights Road today winds through one of the city's most desirable neighborhoods. At the top of the road stands the 1847 William Gilliland log cabin, built by an early resident who probably used this old route. (Then image courtesy of Stan Cohen.)

English engineer Charles Ward moved to Charleston in 1871 and established the Charles Ward Engineering Works a year later. By the 1880s, his successful South Side business had become a leading producer of marine boilers, towboats, tugboats, and ocean-going vessels. After Charles died in 1915, his son Ed took over and operated the business until 1931, when it closed. All that remains of the well-known firm are its boats that still ply the nation's waters—such as the *P. A. Denny*, which used to be a fixture on the Kanawha River. (Then image courtesy of West University Libraries.)

This *c.* 1950 view of the old Kanawha City Bridge shows no less than four service stations at the Thirty-fifth Street and MacCorkle Avenue intersection—including one unidentified station at back right that is advertising gas at 21.9¢ per gallon. In the old days, a service station provided exactly what the name implied—a uniformed attendant filled the tank, checked the oil and belts, cleaned the windshield, and often gave Green Stamps as well. In 1975, the old Kanawha City Bridge was imploded and replaced by the current Thirty-fifth Street Bridge. (Both images courtesy of Jerry Waters.)

From its main line along the South Side, the C&O (CSX) Railroad has provided rail service to the capital city since 1873. The original station was replaced by a second structure around 1890, while the existing depot dates from 1905. It currently includes an upscale restaurant on the upper level and the Amtrak ticket office and waiting room on the lower level. Amtrak operates passenger service three times a week to Chicago and Washington, D.C. (Then image courtesy of Stan Cohen.)

This pair of images from the South Side captures two moments in time that illustrate physical changes over the past century. In 1891, the 1885 capitol and 1886 Ruffner Hotel dominate the skyline, and the working river is not a focal point. The modern photograph includes an interesting combination of old and new architecture in downtown Charleston, which today is a mid-sized capital city that values its riverfront. (Then image courtesy of West Virginia University Library.)

Discover Thousands of Local History Books Featuring Millions of Vintage Images

Arcadia Publishing, the leading local history publisher in the United States, is committed to making history accessible and meaningful through publishing books that celebrate and preserve the heritage of America's people and places.

Find more books like this at
www.arcadiapublishing.com

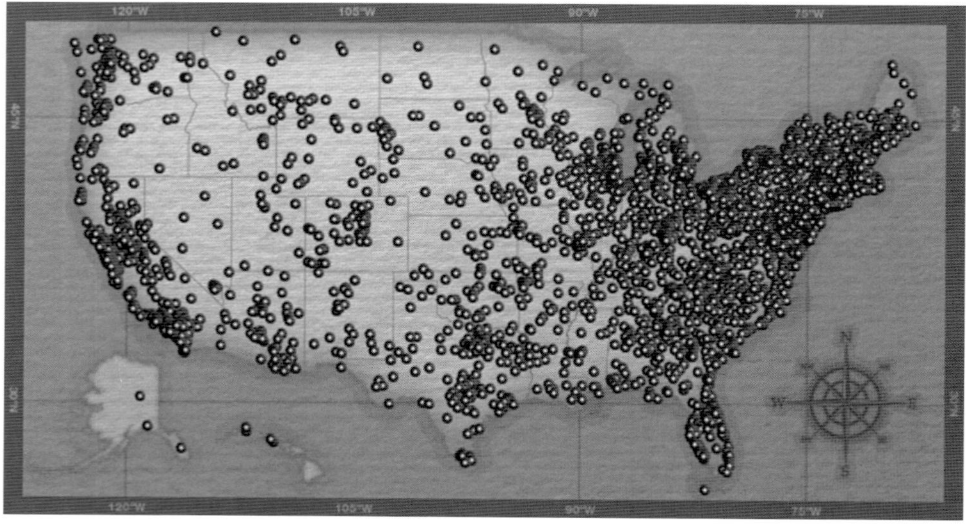

Search for your hometown history, your old stomping grounds, and even your favorite sports team.